Old LARGS

by

R. & M. McSherry

'A Merry Crew'

Heraldic postcards were published in profusion in the Edwardian era; perhaps the sense of identity of a particular city or town was stronger then than now. This coat of arms, which predates the version registered with the Lord Lyon on 4 May 1931, represents the Battle of Largs of 1263. The thistles denote the victorious army of King Alexander III, who repelled the Norwegian invaders from the sea, while the enemy force are represented by a Viking ship with the royal arms of Norway on its sail.

© R. & M. McSherry 1997
First Published in the United Kingdom, 1997
By Stenlake Publishing, Ochiltree Sawmill, The Lade,
Ochiltree, Ayrshire KA18 2NX
Tel/Fax: 01290 423114

ISBN 1 84033 006 6

Thanks are due to the following who have been extremely helpful: The Largs and District Historical Society for the kind use of photographs on pages 7, 9, 22, 25, 28, 29, 32, 33, 36, 41, 43, 44, 47, Mrs Kay McCreadie and Miss Sarah Goldie, and Ian Henderson for use of the picture on page 46.

Introduction

The name Largs is derived from the Gaelic *Learg* meaning a hill slope. The surrounding district is full of historical interest, and archaeological discoveries from the Neolithic and Roman periods have been made. Skelmorlie Aisle, the only remaining relic of the town's ancient church, stands in the old churchyard.

One prominent event connected with the town is the Battle of Largs. This was fought in 1263 between the Scots under King Alexander III, and the Vikings under King Haco. The numerous battle skirmishes ended in victory for the Scots and effectively put an end to the Norwegian claim of sovereignty over the West Coast and Islands of Scotland.

Like most small villages in Ayrshire, handloom weaving was once Largs' main industry. The weavers mainly worked cotton and wool, although some silk work was done for the Paisley mill-owners. Weaving reached its 'golden age' in the nineteenth century, but the development of power looms eventually silenced the 'Weavers' Row' in Gateside Street.

The fishing industry was also important and around fifty boats operated in the area. Small fish stalls were erected along the promenade to sell the freshly caught fish, and boat building also took place, but on a small scale. Largs had a weekly market and four annual fairs where local agricultural produce was sold.

Largs became a police burgh in 1876, and completion of the railway in 1885 put the town within easy reach of Glasgow. Soon new villas were being built by wealthy city business people, along with impressive new churches. These developments contributed to a large increase in the population as people realised how attractive the area was to live in.

Largs' coastal location offers views across the Clyde to the Isles of Cumbrae, the mountains of Arran and the sweeping hills of Argyll and beyond. Two curving bays, both with open grassy foreshores, stretch from the pier, one to the north to the Noddle Burn, and the other passing the Gogo Burn to the Broomlands. The town centre still retains many old buildings, and is dominated by the Main Street along which the A78 from Ardrossan to Greenock runs. There are regular ferry sailings from Largs Pier to the Isle of Cumbrae, and also various excursions to other Clyde resorts by the *P.S. Waverley* and other vessels.

Sport is catered for with two fine scenic golf courses at Routenburn and Kelburn. There are also tennis, bowling, yachting and fishing facilities.

Indoor entertainment is provided at the Barrfields-Vikingar, with the Viking experience, a swimming pool, cinema and regular stage performances.

The town's two main annual celebrations are the crowning of the Brisbane Queen in July and the Viking Week Festival in September. These attract many visitors to the town, especially for the firework display on the final night of the Viking Festival.

Like many of the Firth of Clyde holiday resorts, Largs has seen considerable change over the years, mainly due to the drop in price and increasing popularity of foreign travel. The longer term holiday-makers have now largely been superseded by day-trippers. One popular establishment which has retained much of its originality, however, is Nardini's, a name that is synonymous with both Largs and ice-cream.

Skelmorlie Aisle was converted into a mausoleum in 1636 by Sir Robert Montgomerie in memory of his wife, Dame Margaret. The interior is a fine example of the Renaissance style, with the painted ceiling the work of J.S. Stalker in 1638. The Aisle is now in the care of the Secretary of State for Scotland.

ESPLANADE LARGS.

A quiet early 1900s scene looking north along the esplanade. The Temperance Movement was active in Largs at the time, and the Temperance Hotel occupies a prominent position. The buildings are still recognisable, despite radical changes to their frontages.

Harry Kemp's name was synonymous with entertainment in Clyde resorts from Dunoon to Troon. Many well-known entertainers of the time started their career with him including Tommy Morgan, The Houston Sisters, and Dave Willis. This picture shows his 'Sunny Days' troupe who performed twice nightly in the 1932 Barrfields summer show. Harry Kemp is standing on the right of the back row.

The Curling Hall at the Broomfields was built by Dr John Cairnie in 1813, the same year in which he founded the Largs Curling Club. In 1838 he established the Royal Caledonian Curling Club, which is still the governing body of world curling. Dr Cairnie had the first artificial curling pond to be built in Scotland constructed at the Curling Hall. Two wings were added to the house by Provost John Clark between 1883 and 1889, and in later years it became a hotel. In 1957 it was combined with the adjoining Marine Hotel to become the Marine and Curlinghall Hotel. Sadly both these fine buildings were demolished to make way for flats in 1984.

During the early nineteenth century Largs was well served with curling clubs and artificial ponds for the 'Roaring Game'. The Gogoside pond was floodlit and had a tarmac surface with very little water to freeze, while there was also an artificial pond at Halkshill Club (above). The Largs Thistle Curling Club now has to travel to play at the modern ice rinks in Auchenharvie, Ayr and Irvine.

The new Parish Church of St Columba was built at the foot of Nelson Street in 1812 and demolished in 1890. Two years later the present church was built on its site. Largs' church is mentioned as early as 1250 although it probably pre-dates that to AD 711. From earliest times the church and parish were dedicated to St Columba and the parish church has borne his name for over 700 years. The Scottish Episcopal Church, built in Greenock Road in 1876, is also named St Columba's.

St Columba's Parish Church Sunday School teachers starting out for a trip from the church in 1910. This bus had started operating a public service between Largs and Wemyss Bay in the previous year.

A pierhead scene dominated by the Moorings, designed by architect James Houston in 1936 with an eye-catching nautical look. As well as the fine catering establishment, there was a ballroom on the top floor which was popular with modern dancers, who were entertained by the music of Charlie Harkin and his Kit-Kat Orchestra. The Clyde Coast Bus Stance, which was used extensively by passengers from steamers during the summer months, stood opposite the Moorings.

Nardini's cafe and restaurant, a familiar landmark on the esplanade, was designed by architect James Davidson in 1936 and built in the grounds of Auchenean House. Inside the cafe it's easy to imagine that time has stood still. Much of the original decor has been retained, including the wicker furniture. No trip to Largs is complete without a visit to Nardini's to enjoy their world famous ice-cream.

A postcard produced as a memento of the old Largs pump, which was erected at the Gallowgate in 1801. In 1910 the Gallowgate Well was established on its site with money collected by public subscription. A brick well, designed by architects McMillan and Cronin, was built in 1993 with funding from Ayrshire Enterprise and Cunninghame District Council.

In the winter of 1940 a very heavy snowfall disrupted much of the country and caused high drifts in Largs and throughout North Ayrshire. The problems were compounded when the Fairlie Tunnel was blocked for eleven days by a derailment, closing the rail link in and out of the town. A temporary steamer service was organised from Largs to Wemyss Bay where the train service was still operational. In this picture a horse harnessed to a makeshift sledge loaded with provisions stands outside Nichols Restaurant in Gallowgate Square.

An uninterrupted view of Victoria Esplanade in the early 1900s. The horse-drawn bus is standing at what was for many years the terminus for all types of public transport. In 1951 increasing levels of traffic led to a new bus station being established just off Main Street.

NO. 4067. DESTROYER "LAVEROCK" ASHORE NEAR LARGS, MARCH 1914.   J & R. SIMPSON.

An embarrassing naval disaster prior to the beginning of the First World War. HMS *Laverock* ran aground at the north end of Largs; this picture shows the crew on deck with bystanders and other personnel deciding how to refloat the destroyer.

TURBINE STEAMER
"ATALANTA"
AT LARGS PIER

The Glasgow and South Western Railway's first and only turbine steamer, *Atalanta*, caused considerable interest with 'Doon the Watter' enthusiasts when she visited Largs pier in 1908. *Atalanta* was built by John Brown at Clydebank in 1906 and sailed on many routes on the Clyde (mainly between Ardrossan and Brodick during the winter months). She had a capacity of 1,400 passengers, and her turbine engines were said to have been made experimentally as a model for the *Lusitania*, alongside which she was built. During the Second World War she was renamed *Atalanta* II and used as a troop ship, minesweeper and boom defence ship. She was finally scrapped in 1947 at Methil.

At the turn of the twentieth century travelling people with dancing bears visited towns throughout the country. The bears were chained and made to dance as a form of public entertainment, and few of those who watched them gave little thought for the suffering the animals had to endure. This picture shows gypsies, probably Rumanian, with their bear at Largs on a wet winter's day - which didn't encourage many spectators.

10,684. THE BATHING STATION, LARGS.

The bathing station on the North Esplanade provided changing facilities for bathers at the shingle beach, which was popular with children. Prior to its demolition, the station housed an aquarium and mini zoo for a few years. This was run by Frank Roche who was also a local boat-hirer and delivered the mail to Millport daily.

Hiring boats for fishing and pleasure trips was a popular pastime at the beginning of the century. Numerous boat stations, with fleets of rowing and motor boats, were situated along the esplanade shore. It could be a risky business, however, boarding the boats from what was little more than a floating raft, particularly if the sea was rough.

The model yacht pond at the Broomfields attracted residents and visitors of all ages. Covering half an acre, the pond had a maximum depth of just over a foot, and race lengths varied from twenty-eight to fifty-four yards. In today's world more sophisticated model boats can regularly be seen at the Aubrey Crescent pond, which is used by Largs Model Boat Club. Their flotilla of electronically controlled models makes a fine display.

The old battery in front of the Vandura at the north end of the esplanade, c.1880. It would appear that the young cadets are being instructed on how to manoeuvre the cannon (note the cannon balls lined up against the wall). Many coastal towns had artillery units and Largs was part of the First Ayrshire and Galloway Artillery. They had their headquarters at the Artillery Hall in Seamore Street, demolished in 1991.

Prior to the building of the North Promenade this row of fisherman's huts, known locally as 'the fishboxes', stood on the shore. They were used for selling freshly caught fish, and many years later the boxes were replaced with much smaller versions which boat owners stored their fishing tackle in.

Pierhead, Largs.

5137

A crowded paddle steamer leaving Largs.   The offices of the Glasgow & South Western Railway and the Caledonian Steam Packet Companies are on the right. Today these offices have been replaced by the Cumbraen amusements arcade, which was built in 1955.

THE LARGS GIRL.

The maidens of Largs are O.K.,
They are all nice girls in their way.
They are dainty, petite,
Reserved and discreet,
But I've only seen them by day.

LARGS is a popular watering-place near Fairlie, and has a weather prophet.   A battle once took place at Largs, but the incident is forgotten even by the oldest inhabitant. The Largs Girl is vivacious and pretty.   She cultivates the Gibson Walk and Gorbals dialect.

These comic postcards both date from before the First World War.

Staff pose for a photograph outside J. & R. Simpson's shop in Main Street. Simpson's also had a thriving printing and publishing business and produced a large number of local postcards, some of which are still in circulation. They also ran a lending library, and not to be outdone by the weather even offered an umbrella repair service. The premises are now occupied by a branch of John Menzies.

Union Street around the turn of the century. The villa on the right was called 'Seaview'. It was opened as a girls' home in 1888 by the YWCA, and visited by city shopgirls and others who required a rest due to their long working hours. A short stay at the coast and the healthy seaside air proved beneficial to the visitors' health, and an average of 400 stayed there each year. In 1966 the house was converted into flats and an extension was built joining it to the adjacent Sandringham flats. These were built in 1911, partly on the site of McQuiston's Boatyard.

Main Street looking east. The outline of the buildings has changed very little in the past hundred years. In the nineteenth century an open sewer ran down the middle of the street to the sea.

Largs Golf Club was founded in 1891 and initially played on a nine-hole course at Routenburn before moving to its present site at Kelburn. The Routenburn Club (above) was formally opened by Provost Archibald Boyd. During the First World War the course was used for agricultural purposes, and was subsequently reconstructed by the famous golf professional James Braid. It reopened in 1920. The town council purchased the private house 'Netherpark' as a clubhouse in 1930, and it is now leased by the club from the council.

. Peace Day, Largs . .

Largs' original war memorial in Gallowgate Square. The memorial on the seafront near the Sandringham building was erected and dedicated in 1921. It originally bore the names of eighty-five servicemen from Largs; a further sixty-seven names were added after the Second World War.

THE "CHANTY DYKE," MAIN STREET, LARGS. DEMOLISHED ABOUT 1894.

The 'Chanty Dyke' was situated across from the railway station bordering on Main Street and Aitken Street. The enclosure was used to pen animals which were in transit to and from the ships at the pier or awaiting movement to the local abbatoir.

THE CUMBRAES, BUTE & ARRAN HILLS FROM LARGS.

A. 2289.

The 'Bonny Blink' tearoom was situated on the Haylie Brae, above the gorge on the Largs to Kilbirnie road. With a panoramic view of Largs and the Clyde, it was very popular with motorists and early touring buses.

The bridge across the Gogo Water was swept away during heavy flooding on 20 August 1910. Previous floods had damaged the foundations, but the council had always managed to carry out repair work. The old iron bridge was replaced by a more substantial model in March 1911 and dedicated to the memory of Sir Thomas Makdougall Brisbane. In true Largs style a stall advertising superior ice-cream is visible beyond this improvised log bridge.

The 5th Argyll and Sutherland Highlanders at Holehouse Farm, July 1909. Regimental training camps were held mainly during the summer months, and set up around larger towns throughout the country. This fairly extensive camp had at least 135 bell tents and several large marquees.

Silverae House in Irvine Road got its name from the discovery of a small hoard of silver coins in the area *c.*1840. For many years it was a popular boarding house, but despite the numerous alterations that were made to the original building it closed and was demolished in 1987. It has since been replaced by flats named Silverae Court.

HOLLYWOOD HOME, LARGS

Hollywood Home in Greenock Road was named Underbank when it was built for the Holms Kerr family in 1873. The building was extended in 1936 and renamed the Hollywood Hotel. During the Second World War it was requisitioned by the War Office and became the headquarters of combined operations under the name of HMS Warren. Following the war it was purchased by the Scottish Co-operative Wholesale Society who converted it into a convalescent home. This closed in 1982 and the site has now been developed into modern flats retaining the original names of Hollywood and Underbank.

Laying the memorial stone at the Masonic Temple, Frazer Street, 1910. Founded in 1789, the lodge was granted its charter, No. 173 St John, from the Mother Lodge No. 0 in Kilwinning. Following an agreement in 1807 by the Grand Lodge of Scotland and the Mother Lodge in Kilwinning, charters sanctioning the formation of new lodges were no longer allowed to be issued by Kilwinning. The Largs Lodge celebrated its bicentenary in 1989.

OLD POST OFFICE AND POST GIG ABOUT 1884.

Largs Post Office, which opened at 8 Main Street in 1793, was one of twelve post offices operating in Ayrshire at the end of the eighteenth century. It moved several times before a new office at the corner of Bellmans Close in Main Street was opened in 1905. In 1926 a purpose-built post office was built in Aitken Street and continued to operate there until 1994. The current post office is at 23 Aitken Street, the former office of McSherry & Halliday.

THE GOGO MILL, LARGS

Gogo (above) and Brisbane Mills. The hamlets of 'Newtown of Gogo' to the south of Largs, and 'Brisbane Newtown' to the north, grew to accommodate the workers whose livelihoods depended on the water-powered mills. Weaving, carding and dyeing of flax, wool and linen took place at the mills. Other establishments that harnessed water power included corn, flour, barley and sawmills, but with the development of alternative sources of power the mills became obsolete.

Nelson Street, Largs.

When building began in Nelson Street in the early nineteenth century ancient burial urns were found during excavations at number 73. The houses were originally built for weavers during the industry's boom period, although with the increase in mechanical weaving the trade of the handloom weavers gradually died out. James Boyd of Nelson Street is credited with throwing the last shuttle in 1906. Many of the Nelson Street houses were then used by holiday-makers who rented rooms for the summer. Among some of the famous who once stayed there were the Burrell shipping family of Glasgow, and Sir William Thomson, later Lord Kelvin, who rented Auchenean House while Netherhall was being built.

Brisbane House was originally known as the Mansion House. It was built in 1636 and became home to the Brisbane family from 1671. Their most prominent member, Sir Thomas Makdougall Brisbane, was born in the house in 1773 and served as the sixth governor of New South Wales from 1821 to 1825. The city of Brisbane in Queensland and also a river were named after him. Sir Thomas served as a military general and was also a member of the Royal Society; as a keen scientist he published numerous papers on astronomy. He built Brisbane Academy (now the Stevenson Institute) and presented the Broomlands to the people of Largs. Brisbane House was demolished in the Second World War during commando training exercises, although the oak front door was saved and sent to Brisbane Australia where it can be seen in the City Hall.

BURGH OF LARGS 1876-1936
MISS ENA BAIRD, BRISBANE QUEEN OF LARGS, 1936

The annual crowning of the Brisbane Queen is part of a continuing link between Largs and Brisbane, Australia. The ceremony originated as a Glasgow Fair attraction in 1934 and 1935 when the title was the Carnival Queen. This changed when Miss Ena Baird (left) was crowned Brisbane Queen in 1936. In 1984 the fiftieth anniversary was celebrated when Queen Miss Christina McIntyre (right, with the Warana Festival Queen Mrs Deborah Lucas at the Brisbane GPO Stamp Exhibition) was invited to spend a month in Australia. The present Queen's regalia was presented to Largs by the Government of Queensland.

Sunday afternoon on Largs pier in 1920. The buildings on the esplanade have changed little, although Nardini's is conspicuously absent from this picture. The pier was built in 1834 by the Largs Pier & Harbour Company Ltd. It was strengthened in 1948 and extended a further four-and-a-half feet out to sea. The only major change in recent years has been the addition of the roll-on roll-off landing slip for the Largs-Millport ferry. This service commenced on 11 March 1971 with MV Coruisk and MV Kyleakin II (later named MV Largs).

LARGS FAIR (COLM'S DAY), JUNE 17, 1913.

3069.

In the seventeenth century Largs was granted a charter to hold a weekly market and four annual fairs. The most significant of the fairs was that of St Colms Day, held on the first Thursday after 12 June to celebrate the birthday of St Columba. The fair was attended in great numbers by people from the Highlands and Islands and the surrounding areas, and boats that brought in the livestock were anchored in the bay. While the main object of the fair was originally the sale of livestock (mainly cattle and horses) it was also a time of celebration with singing and dancing.

Heavy flooding took place at Brisbane Road and Glen Road on 22 August 1910 when the Moorburn overflowed. The scene here shows Glenacre Farm with Kelvin Street in the background. Many youngsters appear to be enjoying the floods. Glenacre was a large farm, but like Prospecthill, Chapelton, Gogoside and Flatt was taken over for housing development.

Main Street during the severe storms of 1910.   Shops and buildings were flooded, despite the positioning of flood protection boards.

Founded in 1910, the 1st Largs Scouts were connected jointly with the Clark Memorial and St John's UF Church and registered as the 44th Ayrshire Scout Group. This photograph of the troop, with Scoutmaster G. Coull and Chaplains Rev. J. Geddes and Rev. J.W. Gardner, was taken following the consecration service. The present Largs Scout Group is the 53rd Ayrshire (St Columba's Parish Church).

An early 1890s Largs School class photograph with teacher Miss Jack and pupils. In 1830 Sir Thomas Makdougall Brisbane built and endowed a school in Lade Street named Brisbane Academy. The academy closed in 1893 and the building is better known today as the Stevenston Institute. There were various other schools in Largs including a female school of industry (connected to the parish church), the free school and the local parochial school, but these were small establishments and usually only had one teacher.

The Hills Hotel, Largs.   0329

The Hills Hotel above Burnhouse Road was built in 1876 as a private residence for Mr R. Scott of Scott Clyde Shipbuilders. It remained a private home until the end of the First World War, when it was converted into a hotel. During World War II it was used by the army, reverting back to private use in 1945. For a short time it was occupied by Lord Inverclyde. In 1955 the building was purchased by the King George VI Memorial Trust and formally opened by H.M. The Queen in 1958 as a sports centre. It is now the headquarters of the Inverclyde Scottish National Sports Centre. Continuous development at Inverclyde has made it one of the most modern and well equipped residential sports centres in Britain.